I ENJOY MULTIPLE STREAMS

FINANCIAL SECURITY BRINGS ME JOY

MONEY & BUSINESS

VISION BOARD
Clip Art Book

I GET RICH DOING WHAT I LOVE

I DESERVE A PROSPEROUS LIFE

I ENJOY MULTIPLE STREAMS

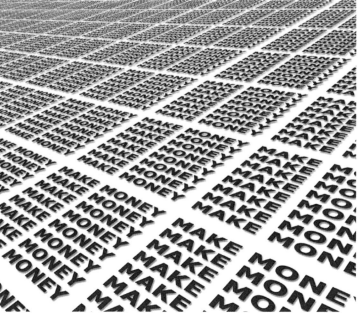

FINANCIAL SECURITY BRINGS ME JOY

I BELIEVE I DESERVE TO BE FINANCIALLY FREE

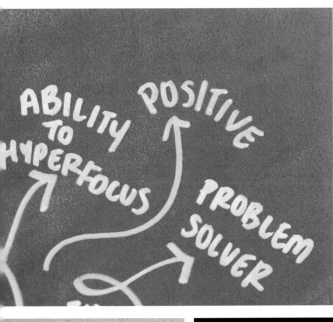

ABILITY TO HYPERFOCUS

POSITIVE

PROBLEM SOLVER

everyday — IS A— FRESH START

YOU'RE THE Best

OPPORTUNITY

BUSINESS

My money goals will manifest this year

impossible

DON'T QUIT

You can WIN if you WANT

YOU WILL DO BIG THINGS

SUPPORT SMALL BUSSINESSES

MY ACCOUNT NEVER STOPS GROWING

HIRING!

LEADERSHIP

SKILLS

Self-employed

My business is overflowing with opportunities

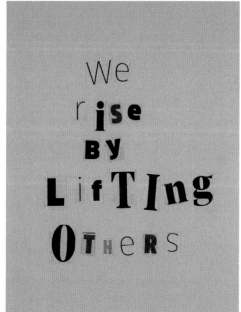

I AM OPEN TO RECEIVING MONEY

Life is Short make it Sweet

Great THINGS take TIME

Every Expert WAS ONCE A Beginner

Enjoy the LITTLE THINGS

DREAM PLAN DO

do not STOP until you're proud

Always BELIEVE in the Impossible

ALWAYS Believe IN THE impossible

Everything I touch turns into gold

BE STRONGER Than Your EXCUSES

ALWAYS STAY HUMBLE AND KIND

I'm Having AN OUT OF Money EXPERIENCE

I'm Broke Please Send Money

Don't Depend On MONEY BUT YOU MUST HAVE A LOT OF MONEY

MONEY Makes MY HEART Go PITTER PATTER

Money is All I Need

Trust Me I'm A BANKER

MONEY IS ABUNDANT TO ME

MASTER money MANIFESTOR

I NEED A Huge AMOUNT OF Money

money Makes The World GO ROUND

I GET RICH DOING WHAT I LOVE

I ACHIEVE MY FINANCIAL GOALS WITH EASE

LOVE
IS HONEY
BUT I WANT
MONEY

I LOVE MONEY AND MONEY LOVES ME

HATE MATH
BUT
LOVE COUNTING
MONEY

WE ARE THE SUM OF THE FIVE PEOPLE

WE SPEND TIME WITH

 this WEEK

 next week

NEXT Month

 goals

 don't forget

 today

 TO DO

 NOTES

 DON'T forget

My finances don't scare me because I have a plan

 TO DO

check list

 Yes

 DO IT

Remember

NO no

IMPORTANT

 Yup!

 GOALS

 THIS WEEK

HOW DO YOU PLAN BETTER?

I DESERVE A PROSPEROUS LIFE

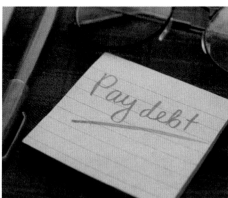

I CAN BECOME FINANCIALLY FREE

I AM CAPABLE OF INCREDIBLE THINGS

EVERYTHING I TOUCH TURNS TO GOLD

MY HARD WORK WILL BRING ME MONEY

I AM MORE THAN MY CURRENT FINANCIAL SITUATION

MY WORK SPEAKS FOR ITSELF

MY MIND IS CLEAR AND I THINK WITH CLARITY

PRESSURE BRINGS OUT THE BEST IN ME

I AM GRATEFUL FOR THE MONEY I HAVE RIGHT NOW

I WILL MAKE MORE MONEY

MONEY IS MY FRIEND, AND I WELCOME IT INTO MY LIFE

I AM AN EXCELLENT MONEY MANAGER

I THINK ABOUT MONEY POSITIVELY

Thank you!

We are thrilled to extend our heartfelt gratitude for your recent purchase of our Money and Business Vision Board Clip Art Book. Your support means the world to us, and we can't wait for you to explore the creative possibilities that await within its pages.

We believe that creating a vision board is an incredible journey towards manifesting your dreams and goals. With this clip art book, we aimed to provide you with a toolkit to make that journey even more exciting and visually engaging. We trust that the vibrant illustrations and versatile elements will empower your vision board to truly reflect your future relationship with money and business.

As you dive into your creative projects, we kindly request your feedback. Your thoughts are invaluable to us and to others who are considering enhancing their creative process with our book. If you have a moment to spare, we would greatly appreciate it if you could share your experience and insights in a few words on Amazon. Your honest review will help fellow dreamers make informed decisions and discover the magic of our **Money and Business Vision Board Clip Art Book.**

Wishing you endless inspiration and success as you craft your money vision board masterpiece!

Warm regards,
Jasmine Eason

Made in the USA
Las Vegas, NV
28 October 2024

10625319R00026